What is hatching?

Bobbie Kalman

🌳 Crabtree Publishing Company

www.crabtreebooks.com

Created by Bobbie Kalman

Author and Editor-in-Chief
Bobbie Kalman

Reading consultant
Elaine Hurst

Editors
Kathy Middleton
Crystal Sikkens

Design
Bobbie Kalman
Katherine Berti

Photo research
Bobbie Kalman

**Production coordinator
and Prepress technician**
Katherine Berti

Photographs
Istockphoto: page 8
Other photographs by Shutterstock

Library and Archives Canada Cataloguing in Publication

Kalman, Bobbie, 1947-
    What is hatching? / Bobbie Kalman.

(My world)
ISBN 978-0-7787-9509-4 (bound).--ISBN 978-0-7787-9534-6 (pbk.)

    1. Eggs--Incubation--Juvenile literature. 2. Animals--Infancy--Juvenile literature. I. Title. II. Series: My world (St. Catharines, Ont.)

QL956.5.K34 2011   j591.4'68   C2010-901975-X

Library of Congress Cataloging-in-Publication Data

Kalman, Bobbie.
  What is hatching? / Bobbie Kalman.
       p. cm. -- (My world)
  ISBN 978-0-7787-9534-6 (pbk. : alk. paper) -- ISBN 978-0-7787-9509-4
(reinforced library binding : alk. paper)
  1. Eggs--Incubation--Juvenile literature. I. Title. II. Series.

 QL956.5.K35 2011
 591.4'68--dc22
                                                                    2010011302

Crabtree Publishing Company

www.crabtreebooks.com   1-800-387-7650

Printed in Hong Kong/042011/BK20110304

Published in Canada
Crabtree Publishing
616 Welland Ave.
St. Catharines, Ontario
L2M 5V6

Published in the United States
Crabtree Publishing
PMB 59051
350 Fifth Avenue, 59th Floor
New York, New York 10118

Published in the United Kingdom
Crabtree Publishing
Maritime House
Basin Road North, Hove
BN41 1WR

Published in Australia
Crabtree Publishing
386 Mt. Alexander Rd.
Ascot Vale (Melbourne)
VIC 3032

Words to know

alligator

bird (chick)

crocodile

duck

egg

hatching

snake

tree

turtle

Hatching is coming out of an **egg**.
Some animals hatch from eggs.
What is hatching from this egg?

egg

A baby **bird** is hatching!

The baby bird is out of the egg.
It is a baby **chick**.

All these baby chicks have hatched.

Did you know that a baby **snake** hatches from an egg?

The baby snake has hatched.
It is climbing up a **tree**.

Did you know that a baby **alligator** hatches from an egg?

These baby alligators have hatched.
They are on their mother's back.

Did you know that a baby **crocodile** hatches from an egg?
This baby crocodile is hatching.

The baby crocodile has hatched.
It is out of its egg now.
It is climbing over some eggs.

Activity

Look at the pictures on these pages.
Which of these things
hatch from eggs?
Which do not hatch?

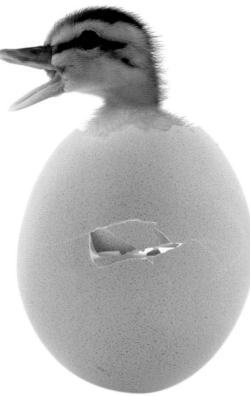

Does a **turtle** hatch
from an egg?

Does a **duck**
hatch?

Does a baby hatch?

Does a tree hatch?

The answers are on the eggs below.

A turtle hatches.

A duck hatches.

A child does not hatch.

A tree does not hatch.

15

Notes for adults

Objectives
- introduce children to the concept of hatching and increase their awareness of the kinds of animals that hatch from eggs

Prerequisites
Arrange for eggs to hatch in your classroom or at your home.
If you cannot hatch real eggs, find a video on the Internet that shows eggs hatching.

Before reading the book
Ask the children:
"What does the word "hatching" mean?"
"How does an animal break out of its egg?"
"Have you ever seen a baby chick hatch?"
"Is a chicken's egg hard or soft?"

Ask the children to pay attention to the pictures in the book. Are all the eggs from which animals hatch hard eggs? Which eggs look soft? Which are the biggest animals that hatch from eggs? (alligators and crocodiles)

Questions after reading the book
Which kinds of animals hatch from eggs?
Introduce the classifications of different kinds of animals:
birds (chickens, ducks)
reptiles (snakes, alligators, crocodiles, turtles)
Which words describe how trees and human babies come to life? (growing from seeds; being born)

Activity: Watch it hatch
Have the children help you incubate eggs to hatch in your class and/or watch videos of different kinds of animals hatching.
Ask the children to draw pictures of an animal of their choice hatching from an egg.

Extensions
Read the books shown below to introduce children to the different ways animals come to life and grow. Both books are *Guided Reading: J*.

For teacher's guide, go to www.crabtreebooks.com/teachersguides